Achieving Organizational Alignment

A Workbook on How to Align Your Organization's Capability and Capacity with the Achievement of Its Strategic Plan Goals

Barry MacKechnie
DoubleBee Publishing

Focus !
Achieve
Barry

Achieving Organizational Alignment

A Workbook on How to Align Your Organization's Capability and Capacity with the Achievement of Its Strategic Plan Goals

DoubleBee Publishing, Inc.

17910 SE 106th Street

Renton, WA 98059

International Standard Book Numbers

ISBN-13: 978-1523880416

ISBN-10: 1523880414

eBook: ISBN: 978-1523880416

Printed in the United States of America

Library of Congress Cataloging-in-Publication Data

MacKechnie, Barry

Achieving Organizational Alignment: Vol. 1 by Barry MacKechnie C.2016. ISBN: 978-1523880416

LCCN: 1523880414

Dedication

As with my first book and its 2nd edition, I dedicate this book to my wife Bette who has supported me as I have advanced through my career and life. With her love and support I have been able to accomplish many wonderful and amazing things.

To Bette,

Be mine forever,

I am forever yours.

Reviews of the Achieving Organizational Alignment Process

....

Barry's process of organizational alignment differentiates itself by facilitating the development of a clear and executable plan that aligns your organization with its business strategy and strategic plan goals.

Doug Ostrom, CEO, Stafford Health Services

....

Barry presents a systematic approach to achieving organizational excellence. The disciplined approach is essential because the concepts are simple but are rarely done well within organizations. Barry's process makes sense of a process that many times we CEOs make too complex.

Anonymous, CEO

....

CEOs must grow into their roles. Their job is to eliminate chaos through wise planning. Wise planning is having a 5-year strategic plan and making Barry's organizational alignment process a habit within your organization. This is the highest and best use of a CEO's time and talent within their organization.

Kevin McKeown, Vistage International, Chair

....

When running a smaller, growing company, it is often hard to look at strategic growth from a pure functional standpoint and not cloud it with the people in place. Barry's organizational alignment process brought to me a clear way to think through our current structure and where we need to focus on capability and capacity as we move forward.

Karey Fey, Pacific Project Management

....

What I found with Barry's process is that it is a very clear and logical pathway to navigate the future of a growing company. He made a complex problem very simple to solve using his organizational alignment process.

Clark Lindsey, CEO, Pacific Project Management

....

Having a thoughtful process on organizational alignment is extremely valuable to me and my team as we go through a high growth mode. We will begin to immediately implement functional role ratings and individual, team, and organization key performance indicators as well as futurizing our organization chart to make sure we have the right people in the right seats.

Kyle Caouette, CFA, CFP, Wealth Management

....

Barry's process methodically gets to the core of what a CEO must do to position their company for growth. Objectively evaluating my organization by each position will help me evaluate our capabilities and align all of our efforts to achieve our goals.

Brett Ferullo, CEO, Northwest Construction

....

In some ways simple, yet with depth and impact, Achieving Organizational Alignment sets an outline and structure to drive improved results. It works!

Bob Foote, President, Canyon Creek Cabinets

....

So many structures in companies are influenced by personalities of the people in the organization. Barry's process of organizational alignment helps senior management evaluate its organization in a more objective and thoughtful way. Futurizing the capability and capacity of your organization is an extremely valuable tool for preparing for the future.

Marty Waiss, President, Investco

....

Barry's process allows a business executive to identify and address underperforming people that are supposed to be fulfilling functional roles. The objective process makes it very easy. The steps to improving your organization become part of your plan to meet your goals.

Jay Sorenson, Principal, Lease Crutcher Lewis Construction

....

Regardless of your organization's current state, Barry's process of organizational alignment ensures a better future state and provides you with the tools for continued development no matter where you want your company to go.

Bill Hill, CEO, Western Integrated Technologies

....

The steps Barry lays out for achieving your organizational goals are exactly what we need to get to the next level. The level of detail he provides in implementing the steps removes any excuses we may have had for not moving forward and achieving our strategic plan goals.

Terry Cook, CEO, The Cascade Group

....

The Achieving Organizational Alignment process forces you to spend less time on being right but rather focuses you on doing what's right for your organization.

Eldon DeHaan, President, WIT

....

Barry's process of strategic alignment and organizational alignment energizes your whole organization to achieve its goals. Success can be achieved at every level. I especially appreciate how this process helps organizations to achieve their goals by taking a complex idea and making it easier. Barry's objective approach is a refreshing change in the way that I try to make our organization more effective. It will help any company achieve its objectives.

Robert Berntson, CEO, Berntson Porter

....

Our management team had, unfortunately, overcomplicated the process of evaluating individual performances in key areas of our business. Barry's functional role review helped us simplify the process, look at key measures objectively, and eliminate barriers that we had created in our own organization. The results have been amazing in both our people and our company's performance.

Jay England, CEO/Owner, Pride Transport

....

About The Author

Barry MacKechnie has more than forty-five years of experience as a business leader, working with CEOs in over five hundred companies and as a business owner and CEO himself. Based upon his extensive experience, Barry has developed a blueprint for executives to follow as they lead their organization through the process of achieving strategic alignment. Barry is the author of the first book in his strategic alignment series, *2nd Edition-Achieving Strategic Alignment*, published in 2013 (over 5000 copies in the hands of CEOs and business leaders around the world). Barry facilitates strategic planning sessions for organizations across the spectrum of industries and leads CEO workshops on achieving strategic alignment throughout the United States and Canada. Barry is a much sought after public speaker on transforming the way businesses work to meet and exceed organizational goals.

Contact Information:

Barry MacKechnie

17910 SE 106th Street Newcastle, WA 98059

Email: barry@ceo-services.com

Phone: 206-399-5698

Website: www.ceo-services.com

Blog: http://www.ceo-services.com/barrysblog

TABLE OF CONTENTS

Achieving Organizational Alignment

A Workbook on How to Align Your Organization's Capability and Capacity with the Achievement of Its Strategic Plan Goals

Introduction

Based on my experience working with over five hundred businesses, I have found that many organizations rise to their own level of incompetence and stay there. Over time, critical positions in the organization are filled by individuals who do not have the capability and/or the capacity to carry out their responsibilities. As a result, those organizations consistently fail to achieve their goals; and, they end up with their teams, at some point, in chaos. By using my process for organizational alignment, organizations no longer experience the calamity caused by not having the right capability and capacity on board when the company goes through critical changes in their business operations.

The purpose of this book is to provide you with a framework for creating an organization that has both the capability and capacity to meet or exceed its future goals, and to avoid chaos.

First, you will learn how to objectively review and rate your current organization's performance.

Second, you will use the objective review to create a plan that will improve your organization's performance in each role.

Third, you will learn how to futurize your organization chart to understand where additional capability and capacity will be required as you drive toward the achievement of your strategic plan goals.

Fourth, you will learn why you need to develop a succession plan for yourself and all of your key positions in your organization.

This book provides you and your organization with a detailed plan for assessing whether or not your current organization has the capability and the capacity to achieve its strategic plan goals. After completing the analysis of your organization you are provided with the necessary tools to plan how and when your organization will need to change in order to achieve your goals.

Growth without capability and capacity throughout your organization will result in chaos. Using the tools and concepts in this book will help you align your organization's resources so that you can achieve your strategic plan goals without chaos.

The majority of the goals created during the strategic planning session involve growth. Growth puts a strain on any organization, will test an organization's strengths, and will expose its weaknesses.

The key to the future success of an organization depends on the capability and capacity of every team and the members of those teams.

I have been utilizing the framework presented in this book to provide guidance to organizations as they look into their future and grow their business. It has consistently proven to be a successful approach for evaluating and aligning an organization's ability for achieving its strategic plan goals. Once you have completed this book, you, too, will know how to change your organization into a high-performance team that consistently achieves your strategic plan goals.

Chapter One

Aligning Your Company with Your Strategic Plan Goals

Key things to have in place:

1. A strategic plan for the next five years with goals that have been validated and tested for reality and achievability during your strategic planning session
2. Action items that, once completed, will drive your organization to the achievement of strategic plan goals
3. A leadership group that is committed to sustaining the pursuit of a strategically aligned organization and that holds itself and the organization accountable for achieving its strategic plan goals
4. An organization that thrives on accountability and is committed to reaching its strategic plan goals

These four key elements, the subject of my book *2nd Edition-Achieving Strategic Alignment,* must be accomplished prior to starting the process outlined in this book. *Achieving Strategic Alignment* provides organizations with a detailed plan for setting goals and then driving the achievement of those goals down through the organization. I encourage you to read that book if you haven't already. Creating and reviewing those long-term goals is accomplished during a two-day strategic planning session, which is dedicated to setting the future goals for the organization.

Utilizing my five-year method for goal setting, you and your team define your goals for the next five years. In my experience, a vast majority of goals are focused on the following four key financial measurements:

- Revenues
- Gross Margin
- Overhead
- Profit

These goals become the over-arching key performance indicators for the organization. As you begin to evaluate the performance of your organization, these key performance indicators are a critical element to the process. Most companies get this wrong. When I talk to them about their key performance indicators, they will identify ten, fifteen, twenty, or even more key performance numbers that they track. When I lead them through a discussion about their key performance indicators, they quickly realize that the majority of the key performance indicators they have identified are subsets of the four major goals of revenues, gross margin, overhead, and profits. One of the outcomes of your strategic planning retreat is that you must identify your key performance indicators and their subsets. This is an important concept to understand; please see Appendix A where you will find a detailed discussion on key performance indicators and their subsets.

I dedicated a full chapter in my first book on why strategic plans fail. The most common reasons for failure to achieve strategic plan goals are lack of leadership, lack of consistent follow-up, and the organization's response to the need for change. For the first two (leadership and consistent follow-up), the CEO affirms the commitment of the organization to achieving its strategic plan goals by stressing the importance of completing every action item identified during the strategic planning session. The CEO's leadership and consistent follow-up needs to be sustained until all goals are achieved.

That leaves the third element of why strategic plans fail—people. The people part of the formula is the focus of this book. With a set of validated, tested, reality-based, and achievable strategic plan goals in place, the organization then needs to examine its own ability to achieve those goals. The steps you need to take include:

1) Objectively review your current organization's performance (chapters 2-3)

2) Create a plan that will improve your organization's performance in each role (chapter 4)

3) Futurize your organization chart to understand where additional capability and capacity will be required as you drive toward the achievement of your strategic plan goals (chapter 5)

Chapter Two

Current Organization—Identifying Basic Functional Role Responsibilities

With your strategic plan goals set, you must begin the process of objectively evaluating the performance of your current organization.

Functional Role Organization Chart—Assessing Your Organization Today

The first step toward achieving a strategically aligned organization is to determine how well your organization is performing today. This is done by creating a simple organization chart based on the functional roles within your organization. Functional roles are defined by what that role is supposed to be delivering to the organization. The important point is that you describe the role by what it is supposed to provide, which may be different from what the role is currently providing. No names of individuals should be put on this basic organization chart. A functional role review is meant to be objective not judgmental. The tendency is to want to add an individual's name into the process. Don't do that during the functional review. It clouds the process because the addition of someone's name taints the process with subjectivity. We'll delve into the individual's part of the process after we complete the objective functional role review.

This should not be an overly complicated process. Just use a blank piece of printer paper and hand draw your functional role organization chart. Here's a simple organization chart with a functional role title in each box:

Figure 2.1 Basic Functional Role Organization Chart

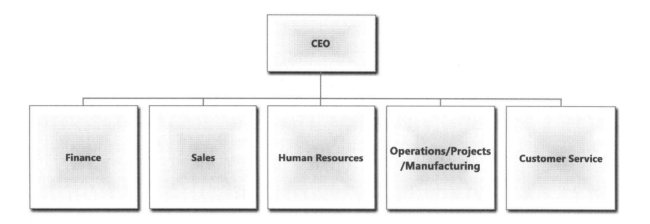

As you can see in this example, no names are inserted; only the functional roles are listed.

Under each functional role box, create a broad description of what the role is supposed to deliver to the organization. This should be done in broad concepts for each role description. For the basic functional roles in Figure 2.1, the role descriptions could be as follows:

Finance: Responsible for the financial health of the company. Provides timely reporting to all departments. Manages cash flow and banking relationships. Assures adequate capital reserves and monitors and manages overhead expenses.

Sales: Responsible for achieving all sales goals including current client sales levels, increasing current client sales volumes, customer relationships, customer retention, and adding new customers in order to reach the sales growth and gross margin goals of the company. Manages sales related overhead expenses.

Human Resources: Responsible for recruiting and hiring top quality employees, providing training, managing employee benefits programs, and keeping employee retention levels above industry average. Helps manage payroll costs, defines employee benefit plans, and manages human resource related overhead expenses.

Operations/Projects/Manufacturing: Responsible for the production of all offered products and for manufacturing those products in a timely manner. Responsible for gross margins on manufactured products, labor and material costs, and inventory levels. Manages manufacturing related overhead expenses.

Customer service: Responsible for handling all customer communications regarding warranties, product delivery, claims, and product support. Assists sales with customer retention efforts and manages customer service related overhead expenses.

Once you have identified and defined the functional roles of your organization, you now need to rate the delivery of each of those functional roles. The rating system is a scale of 1-10, with a 10 identified as a role that never fails in its delivery, always sees problems before they occur, and ensures that every detailed function within its operations is delivered without fail, ever. I have worked with over five hundred companies and have never seen a 10 rating for a functional role.

You can rate the functional delivery of each role by yourself, or you can have your leadership team involved in this step. I have found that it serves the organization best if you go through this process as a group with your executive team. During the strategic planning retreats that I facilitate I take the strategic planning team through this process. It is much more objective when it is done as a group and the feedback is honest and helpful for all of the participants. Everyone contributes to the rating so results are a fair assessment of the functional role delivery.

The next step is to add up all of your ratings and divide it by the number of role boxes to get the averaged rating for your organization. In the example in Figure 2.2, the functional rating of this organization is 6.8 (34 divided by 5). This is the average for the organization and should be entered in the CEO box as seen in Figure 2.2 below.

Figure 2.2 Basic Functional Role Organization Chart with Ratings

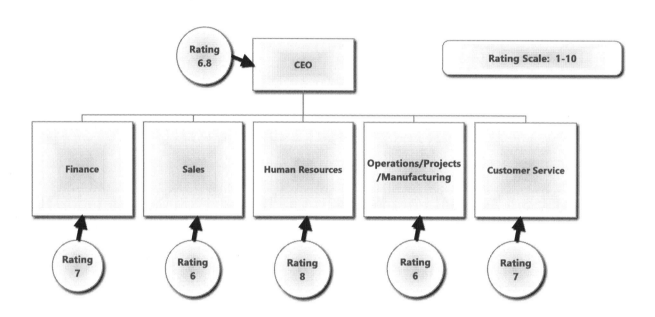

I have found that most organizations have an average rating below 7. The goal of achieving organizational alignment is to get all of your functional role deliverables to a 9 rating. In Figure 2.2, achieving a 9 rating represents a 32 percent improvement in functional role delivery. I have observed that most organizations have managed to get to where they are as a business with a functional role rating of less than 7. Most of those organizations have been evidencing some form of breakdown in their performance. Growth creates stress points in an organization. The goal is to eliminate the roadblocks to growth by improving performance. Using this functional role rating process initiates the path to improvement. Imagine the power of your organization if you are able to improve your total functional role delivery to a 9 level. The outcome is that you will have a clear competitive advantage in your marketplace. You will have a high performance team focused on achieving your strategic plan goals. That is the goal of achieving organizational alignment.

The basic functional role analysis provides a foundation from which a plan will be created to improve your ratings to at least a 9 level.

Chapter Three

Detailed Review of Your Functional Roles

Use your basic functional role review chart as a platform to move into the next phase of organizational alignment. This step delivers a more detailed review of each functional role, which provides you with a starting point to determine where and how you and your team need to focus your efforts to improve from your current rating level to a 9+ rating.

Each of the functional roles can be further defined by the detailed tasks it is supposed to deliver. Using the basic functional role chart created in 2.1, you can add details that define what the role should be accomplishing as depicted in Figure 3.1. The detailed functions should include all of the daily responsibilities of each functional role. Again, no names of individuals should be put on this basic organization chart. This process is objective not judgmental. A functional role review is meant to be objective. The tendency is to want to add an individual's name into the process. Don't do that during the functional review. It clouds the process because the addition of someone's name taints the process with subjectivity.

Figure 3.1 is an example of what the detailed functional role chart should look like.

Figure 3.1 Detailed Functional Role Chart

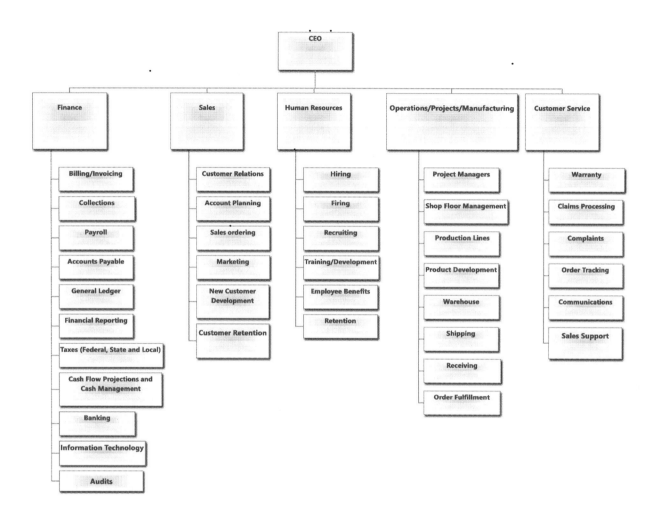

18

Once you have completed your detailed functional role chart, you will utilize the same rating system of 1-10 to rate the delivery of each detailed functional role.

Figure 3.2 Detailed Functional Role Chart with Ratings

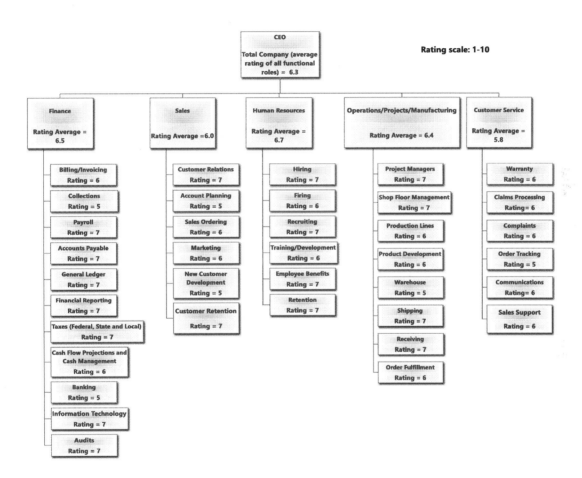

Using the same method you used in the first phase functional role analysis, add up all of the ratings for each functional role and divide the total by the number of detailed functions to get the average rating for that functional role. For example, Human Resources had six detailed functions that added up to a total of 40; therefore, the average for Human Resources is 6.7. Compared with the initial functional role rating of 8.0 for Human Resources (Figure 2.2), the detailed role rating resulted in a lower rating for Human Resources. In my experience, the results of the detailed functional role ratings will be different than the initial rating. Some will go up, and some will go down. Rating the tasks that are supposed to be completed provides a much closer look at role delivery, which can change the initial rating and reflect a more accurate assessment. Add up the new averages from the detailed functional reviews, and divide that by the number of functional role boxes in order to get the organization's average that goes in the CEO box. In Figure 3.2, the functional role averages were 6.5 + 6.0 + 6.7 + 6.4 + 5.8 = 31.5/5 = 6.3.

The next step is to take the detailed functional role and highlight the areas that are less than 7. These are the most immediate areas you need to improve. In Figure 3.3, if each functional role were improved to a 7, by focusing on training, processes, or procedures, the organization would have improved its functional role delivery by over 11 percent.

Figure 3.3 Detailed Functional Role Chart with Ratings and Immediate Areas for Improvement

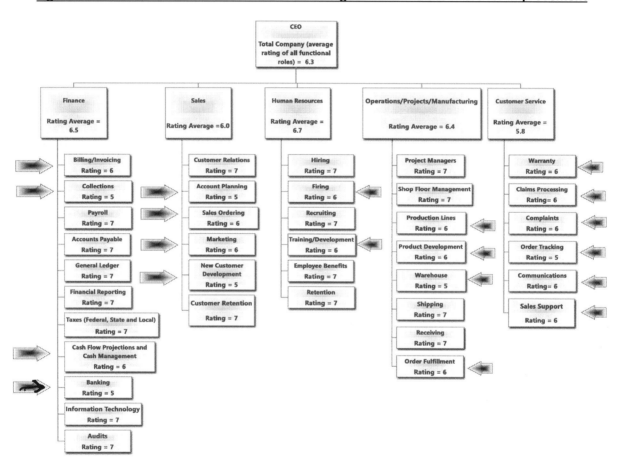

With the detailed functional role analysis completed, we now have a roadmap to make improvements in the operations. The goal is to achieve a 9 rating level for the entire organization.

Chapter Four

Functional Role Improvement Plans—Improving Performance of Individuals

Up to this point in the process, the names of people have been kept off of the organization charts in order to keep the evaluation as objective as possible. So far, the process has utilized this objective evaluation in order to determine where the organization is today and to identify areas where it is possible to accomplish immediate improvement. The long-term goal of getting each functional role delivery to a 9 rating will require two more steps. Now it is time for you to assign names to each functional role detail. Wherever there is a functional role delivery rating of less than 7, as noted by the arrows in Figure 3.3, the person who is delivering that function needs to be put on a path of immediate improvement.

Figure 4.1 Detailed Functional Role Chart with Ratings and Immediate Areas for Improvement—with Names

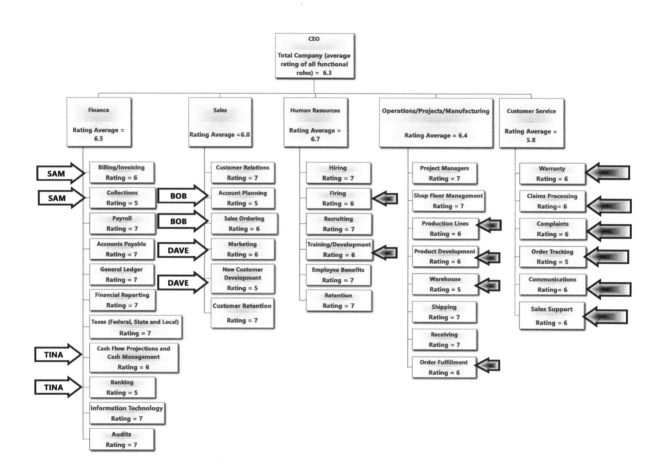

Now it is time to develop a plan for each functional role that includes a detailed program for improving the rating from its current level to a rating level of 9. In Figure 3.3, we noted the segments of a functional role that were being delivered at a very low level. These are the areas that need immediate attention. In Figure 4.1 above, a few names have been added. Your chart will have names for every function that is rated at below a 7. The purpose of this review and the following discussions is to objectively examine the capability of every employee to fulfill their functional role and to deliver it at a 9 level.

You need to identify who is delivering the individual functional role segments so that you can create a plan that will help them improve the delivery of their functional role.

In working with hundreds of companies, I know how difficult it is to make sure the right people are in the right positions within your organization. Many times, people are promoted because of tenure. Sometimes people end up with an expanded position because no one else wanted to take on the additional responsibilities. Over time, friendships form that can cloud business decisions. Because of these things, the organization ends up with people in roles they cannot perform successfully. This part of the organizational alignment process helps to clearly assess whether or not your people are successfully fulfilling their roles.

The next step in the process involves providing each employee with a plan on how they can improve their functional role delivery. When we have completed that step, we will have developed improvement plans for each detailed functional role.

Functional Role Improvement Plan—Executive Team

The best place to start is with the executive team. I have found that a very positive way to complete this process for the executive team is to have the entire executive team help fill out the functional role improvement form together. The process must be fair, honest, and positive. Don't allow statements, such as "why can't you get that done," into the conversation. Keep it positive by focusing on how you can help each other improve. Keep the focus on solving the problem of trying to get the organization to a functional role delivery rating of 9.

Gather your executive team together with a blank functional role improvement form for each of their functional roles. Have members of the executive team work together completing the position description, strengths, and weaknesses; make suggestions on how the weaknesses can be eliminated. It is a healthy process for your executive team. Each member gets great feedback from peers. They see how the rest of the team relies on them for their strengths, how their peers understand where the weaknesses are, and how they can help each other overcome those weaknesses. It is not uncommon to find that a member of your executive team is strong in most areas but is failing to deliver one function as successfully as it could be delivered by another team member. By delegating that function to someone else you enable the executive to focus on what they do best, their strengths. This follows the concept that I utilize over and over with executives and executive teams. The concept is "the highest and best use" of one's time and talent. As an example: A sales manager may be very good at business development through their community and industry relationships. He or she may not be good at completing the paperwork for their position. The highest and best use of this sales manager is to free them up from the paperwork and let them have more time developing community and industry relationships that will lead to more sales. Handing off the paperwork to a sales assistant will eliminate the weakness in the sales manager's functional role delivery. Having the executive team work together to complete the functional role improvement form for each of their own roles makes them a stronger team and it solves the problem of how to get the executive team's functional role delivery rate to a 9 or better.

Figure 4.2 is an example of the functional role improvement form that I utilize with my clients:

Figure 4.2 Functional Role Improvement Form

Name Position Description Current Functional Role Rating #_____ Key Performance Indicator(s):			
Functional Role Description	**Strengths**	**Weaknesses**	**Plan to provide coverage for the weaknesses**

Figure 4.3 is an example of the functional role improvement form for the CEO position.

Figure 4.3 CEO Functional Role Improvement Form

Name: CEO			
Position Description: Responsible for providing the company with leadership and vision. Achievement of strategic plan goals. Current Functional Role Rating #__6.3_____ Key Performance Indicator(s): Profit			

Functional Role Description	Strengths	Weaknesses	Plan to provide coverage for the weaknesses
Provide overall leadership to the executive team. Establish strategic plan goals and communicate those goals to the entire organization. Develop a high performance executive team that achieves the organizations goals consistently. Provide financial resources to assure a sustainable organization that continually achieves its goals	Business development	Doesn't spend enough time in the marketplace	Delegate project management to operations manager. Book 25-30 hours per week in calendar for meetings with existing clients and targeted new businesses.
	Estimating and bidding on projects		Spend 8-10 hours per week with estimating department. Bring in projects and hand off to estimating for bidding
Key Performance Indicator: 10 percent profit	Managing bank relationship		Work with Chief Financial Officer to hand off some of the

25

			daily routine connections with the bank
	Managing client relationships		Spend 25-30 hours per week with clients
		Project details—lacks extended focus	Operations manager responsible for all project management
		Managing people—lacks consistent follow through, doesn't like the details	Operations manager and Chief Financial Officer to provide people management of administration staff and all field operations
	Financial review of company	Spends too much time doing this.	Set up KPIs with the Chief Financial Officer and develop a dashboard daily report that communicates operations. Chief Financial Officer working with operations manager to set and utilize processes for collecting and reporting of daily field data.
		After setting goals, managing key personnel in meeting those goals	Have weekly meeting with Chief Financial Officer and operations manager to validate goals and adequacy of resources

Functional Role Improvement Plan—All Employees

The next step is for the executive team to begin working with all employees on their team and the functional role that each delivers. Complete a functional role improvement form that details the responsibilities of that functional role. The form will also have key performance indicators that provide a benchmark for an objective analysis of how a role is being delivered.

As your leaders complete each position review for your entire organization a functional role improvement form should be completed by the person to whom the employee reports. If you are the CFO you will do this for every member of the financial team who reports directly to you. If you are the sales manager, you will complete this for all sales team members who report directly to you. This process should be completed by each person who has an employee or group of employees that they lead. You should work on the functional role improvement form for the employee that reports directly to you. You should do this on your own and then review it with each employee. Do not let the employee fill this out for their own position. Very seldom are they as objective as you will be. Most employees like to believe they are doing a great job when, in fact, they may only be fulfilling their role at a 5 level. Remember—you need them to be at a 9 level.

The form should include key performance indicators that can be utilized to objectively assess the delivery of each segment of the functional role. Write in the strengths of that employee and the weaknesses of that employee that have been demonstrated as they deliver their role responsibilities. Write down your thoughts about how the weaknesses can be improved either through mentoring, internal training, or external training/education programs. You may decide that it is better to hand off some of the role responsibilities that are an apparent weakness for this employee, to another employee who has strengths in delivering that role responsibility.

Once you have completed the functional role improvement forms for your direct report employees, your next step is to meet with those employees and review their functional role improvement form. This is best accomplished in a one-to-one meeting where you start the meeting describing the process the entire organization is completing with the goal of achieving organizational alignment. Explain in detail the functional role review of the entire company and the detailed review of each segment of a functional role and the ratings that were given for the current delivery of those segments. Let the employee know that this is an organization-wide initiative and that every employee's role is being reviewed in the same manner. Restate the goal of getting the company to a functional role delivery rating of 9 overall. During this meeting, your discussion should focus on how you can help the employee improve their weaker areas and how that will benefit the organization. Don't let the meeting turn into a defensive explanation by the employee. Make sure they understand this is a process for improving the entire organization and that everyone is going through the same process. Keep it positive. Keep it fair. Keep it focused on solving the problem of how the entire organization can achieve an overall functional role rating of 9 or better.

The detailed role delivery rating process identifies areas that need improvement. The ensuing discussion with the employee helps identify where and how improvements can be made. As an example, let's continue the review of Sam in Collections. During the discussion with Sam, he explains that it is impossible to get the collection cycle down to forty-five days because it takes over twenty days to get the invoices from the sales team. The red flag was poor collections but the identified area that needs improvement is in the sales invoicing process. The rating for Sam may change because of your detailed discussions, and the new area of focus is the sales invoicing process. That is the purpose of this role improvement process. Identify the problem and implement a solution.

A plan for the employee's improvement should be developed during this meeting with dates for each of the steps to be completed by and key performance indicators that will be utilized to track their improvement. Budgets and resources should also be identified if the employee's plan calls for external training programs. Many companies decide that they want to sponsor those external programs by paying for the employee to successfully complete a training curriculum with a certification or grade achievement level to be achieved by the end of the program.

This may also prompt the organization to bring in a training program if it is determined that several employees could benefit from a similar curriculum. Many leadership development programs have already been designed for delivery to an organization.

During the functional role review process your discussions may lead you to the conclusion that the employee cannot successfully deliver their functional role. Your planning must also include whether the undeliverable portions can be handed off to other employees and whether or not there are other areas where the company can better utilize the strengths of that employee. The other conclusion may be that there is not a good fit within the organization for that employee and that they must be terminated.

The entire process of functional role review is completed when you review the form with each employee. The focus is on the delivery of functional role responsibilities at a 9 level or higher for the entire organization. Identify key performance indicators and specific subset key performance indicators for each functional role. As an example, in the hypothetical company referenced for the sample charts included here, Sam, who is in charge of collections (Figure 4.1), is rated at a 5. Let's say, in this instance the normal collection period for outstanding invoices for the industry is forty-five days, but it is taking Sam sixty days. When collections are slow, the company has to draw from its line of credit. That increases their interest expense, which is an overhead expense. By reducing the collection period by fifteen days the company could reduce its interest expense, which will reduce their overhead expense. The subset key performance indicator for the collections position is a forty-five-day average collection cycle and reduced interest expense from the line of credit. This becomes the goal of the functional role for Sam, and these two key performance indicators will be added to his role improvement form.

The goal is to achieve improved operations, revenue growth, or other key initiatives by improving the effectiveness of every employee in their current position. In our example company, improving its organization's functional role delivery from a 6.8 to a 9.0 rating level is a 32 percent increase in productivity. That level of improvement will increase the profitability of an organization. It will also position the organization for future growth since its foundation is a strong team that is delivering each role at a 9 level.

These same results will improve your organization's capability for growth and impact your capacity for growth since a 32 percent improvement in functional role performance will not require additional employees as your organization grows its revenues. Having a strategically aligned organization will provide you with a distinct competitive advantage. Your high-performance organization will be able to outperform your competitors. Having that competitive advantage will allow you to take market share away from you competitors.

Chapter Five

Building Your Organization for the Future—Adding Capacity and Capability

Now that you have completed the functional role improvement process, it is time to plan for the future of each functional role. I refer to this process as futurizing your organization chart. This step in the process focuses on making sure you identify when and where your growth will require new capabilities (talent/experience) and where your growth will require additional capacity (more people to get the job done). Strategic planning is not only about setting goals. It also involves making sure that your organization is prepared to grow and improve as it achieves its future strategic plan goals. Growth causes stress for an organization. The process of futurizing your organization chart will identify where and when those stress points will occur. This will help you manage the addition of capacity and capability as your strategic plans are achieved. Growth without forward vision creates chaos. Futurizing your organization chart provides you with that forward vision and eliminates that chaos. In the example that I use, the organization is adding capability and capacity for growth. When the economy is indicating that it could be heading into a business downturn, you should also use this process to identify where you will make reductions in capacity if a few years in your 5-year strategic plan have been forecasted to result in a decline in business. This futurizing of your organization should be done during your strategic planning retreat at the same time that you are setting your strategic plan goals. Your organization and your strategic plan need to be aligned.

In chapter 3, Figure 3.1 (copied below as Figure 5.1), we listed the organization's functions. The next step is to now take that same functional role organization chart and estimate how many people are involved in completing each function. As an example, under the finance role there is an accounts payable box. If you have a full-time person processing and paying vendor invoices, then write "1" (one full-time employee) in the box for that role function. If you have two accounts payable clerks, then write "2" in the box for that role function. In the sales department, if you have fifteen employees working in sales and they perform all of the sales role functions, then write "15" in the top "Sales" box. Complete this process for your organization as it is today. Once you have added all of the role functions and included the number of full time people for each group, put that number in the top box for that group. Make sure you have added the functional role leader to the headcount. In our example for Sales, we have 15 employees performing all of the functional roles within sales. The number "16" will appear in the "Sales" box since we need to add the functional role leader for the sales team. Here's an example of what you will end up with when you complete this step. Our example in Figure 6.1 has seventy-two employees who report up through the organization structure to the CEO, including the CEO.

Figure 5.1 Functional Roles (detailed) with Full-Time Employees

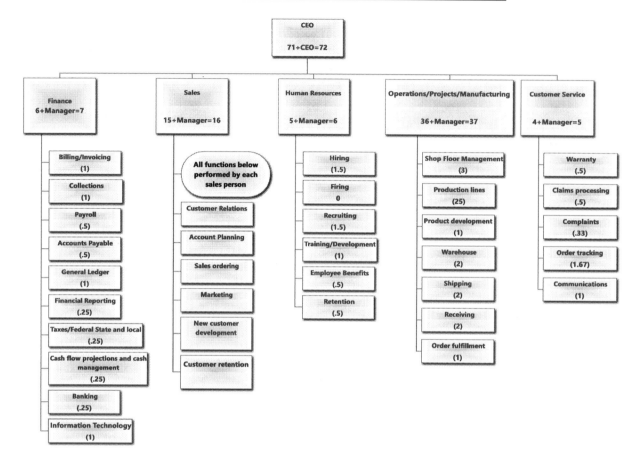

This is your baseline organization from a functional role level.

Futurizing Your Organization Chart

Using this baseline organization structure (Figure 5.1), you now need to begin stepping into the future and looking at where growth will impact your organization chart. This time, you are only looking at adding capacity in the areas where growth will put stress on the ability of a group to be able to sustain its high level of activity as the company grows. Without added capacity, processes begin to break down. Once processes break down inside of a functional group, that role becomes a roadblock to the achievement of company goals.

For purposes of our discussion, let's say that the strategic planning group validated that the company could easily increase its top line revenues of fifty million by 20 percent the first year, by 20 percent the second year, and by fifteen percent the third year, while maintaining its gross margin percentage. Each functional role will be impacted by that growth and will require added capacity or new skills. Let's go through each functional role and decide where and when added capacity will be needed, and estimate how much it will cost to add that capacity or new skill.

32

Figure 5.2 Added Capacity Plan

Department	1st Year of Plan	2nd Year of Plan	3rd Year of Plan
Finance			
Billing Clerk		.5	.5
Cost		$20,000	$20,000
Payroll Clerk	1.0		1.0
Cost	$45,000		$47,000
Total Cost for Finance	**$45,000**	**$20,000**	**$67,000**
Sales			
Sales	2.0	2.0	2.0
Cost	$150,000	$155,000	$155,000
Total Cost Sales	**$150,000**	**$155,000**	**$155,000**
Human Resources			
Recruiter	1.0		1.0
Cost	$50,000		$50,000
Total Cost HR	**$50,000**		**$50,000**

Department	1st Year of Plan	2nd Year of Plan	3rd Year of Plan
Operations			
Shop Floor Manager	1	1	
Cost	$110,000	$110,000	
Production Personnel	5	5	5
Cost	$250,000	$250,000	$250,000
Warehouse, Shipping, and Receiving	3	3	3
Cost	$150,000	$155,000	$160,000
Inventory Manager (new position)	$75,000		
Total Cost Operations	**$585,000**	**$515,000**	**$410,000**
Customer Service			
Service Agents	2	2	2
Cost	$65,000	$70,000	$70,000
Total Cost Customer Service	**$65,000**	**$70,000**	**$70,000**
Total Cost	**$850,000**	**$740,000**	**$685,000**

By putting these changes into the organization's structure for the next three years, you can see what your expanded organization looks like, when you have to hire, and how much it will cost. This process of building your future organization chart is best done with the entire executive team working on each section.

This process should be completed during your strategic planning retreat. During your strategic planning session, you created the company's goals. At this point of your strategic planning session, usually the second half of day two, each functional role leader is asked to estimate when they will need to add capacity and/or capability as the organization achieves those goals. I use a flip chart for each functional role. When the entire organization is completed I put all of the flip charts onto a wall with functional roles aligned with the original organization chart. You can accomplish the same thing by completing the futurizing of your organization using a single sheet of paper for each functional role. After you have completed the futurizing of each functional role you can take the sheets of paper and shape them into your organization chart. Here are some examples of functional role plans for the next three years of an organization. At the end, I have merged them all into a single organization chart that shows the company growing from 71 employees to 115 in three years.

Futurized Organization Chart
Functional Role: Finance
Figure 5.3

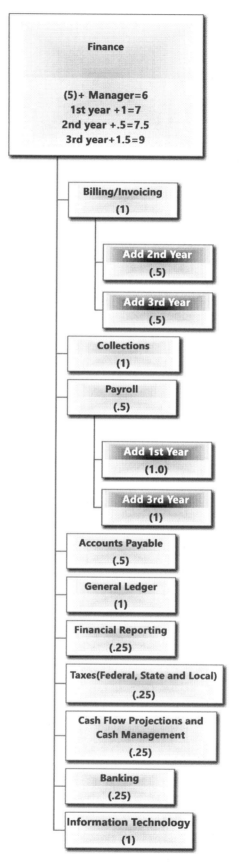

Finance

(5)+ Manager=6
1st year +1=7
2nd year +.5=7.5
3rd year+1.5=9

Billing/Invoicing
(1)

Add 2nd Year
(.5)

Add 3rd Year
(.5)

Collections
(1)

Payroll
(.5)

Add 1st Year
(1.0)

Add 3rd Year
(1)

Accounts Payable
(.5)

General Ledger
(1)

Financial Reporting
(.25)

Taxes(Federal, State and Local)
(.25)

Cash Flow Projections and
Cash Management
(.25)

Banking
(.25)

Information Technology
(1)

Futurized Organization Chart
Functional Role: Sales
Figure 5.4

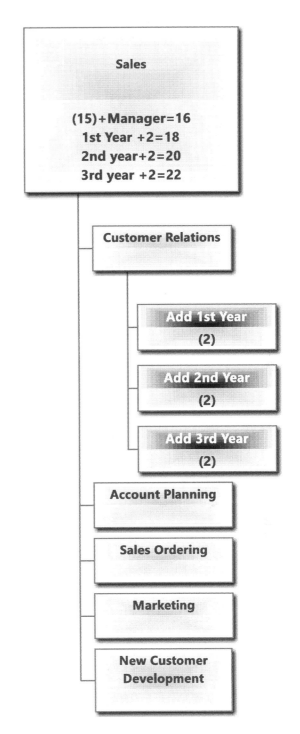

Futurized Organization Chart
Functional Role: Human Resources
Figure 5.5

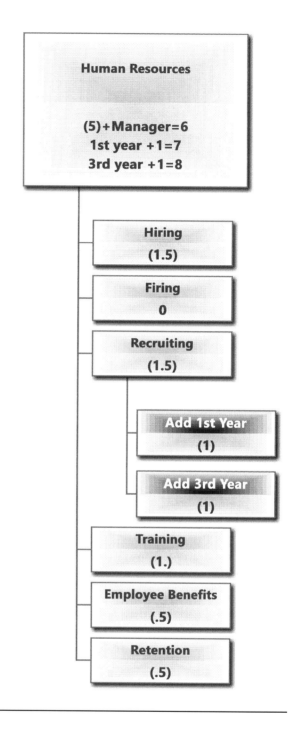

Futurized Organization Chart
Functional Role: Operations
Figure 5.6

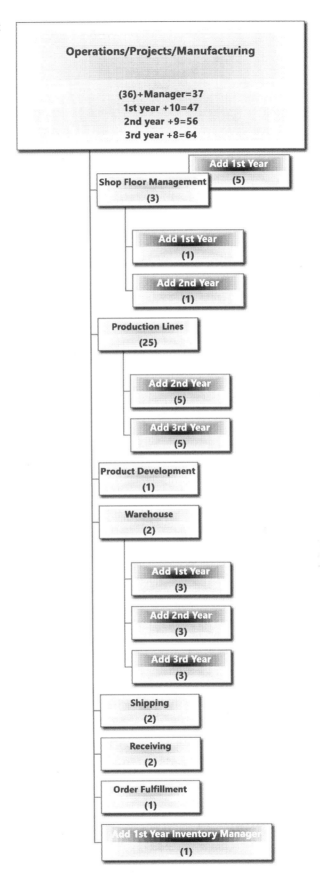

Operations/Projects/Manufacturing

(36)+Manager=37
1st year +10=47
2nd year +9=56
3rd year +8=64

Shop Floor Management (3)

Add 1st Year (5)

Add 1st Year (1)

Add 2nd Year (1)

Production Lines (25)

Add 2nd Year (5)

Add 3rd Year (5)

Product Development (1)

Warehouse (2)

Add 1st Year (3)

Add 2nd Year (3)

Add 3rd Year (3)

Shipping (2)

Receiving (2)

Order Fulfillment (1)

Add 1st Year Inventory Manager (1)

Futurized Organization Chart
Functional Role: Customer Service
Figure 5.7

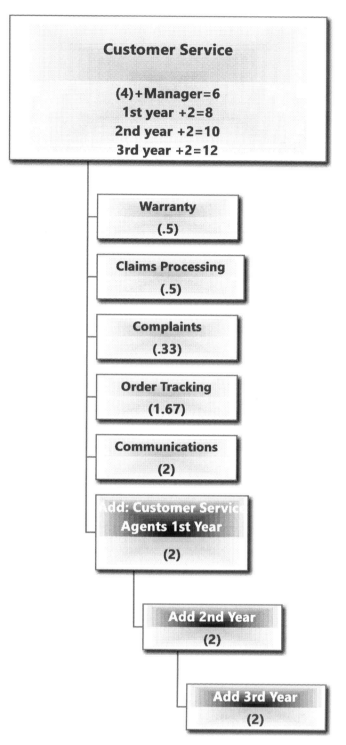

Customer Service

(4)+Manager=6
1st year +2=8
2nd year +2=10
3rd year +2=12

Warranty
(.5)

Claims Processing
(.5)

Complaints
(.33)

Order Tracking
(1.67)

Communications
(2)

Add: Customer Service
Agents 1st Year
(2)

Add 2nd Year
(2)

Add 3rd Year
(2)

Figure 5.8 is the futurized organization chart after combining all of the functional role organization charts into a single chart:

Figure 5.8 Futurized Organization Chart

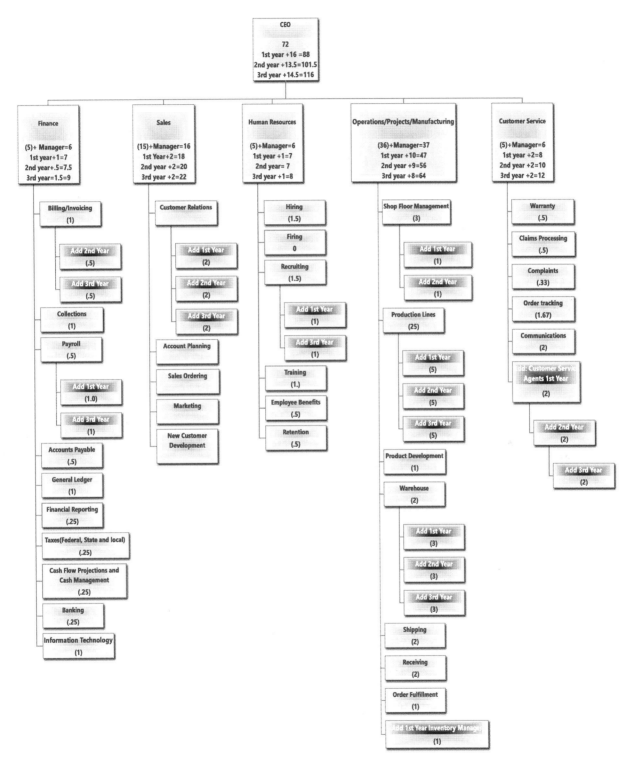

Now you can see the future capability and capacity of your organization. You have a visual representation of what it will take from a capacity standpoint to achieve your strategic plan goals.

If there is a forecasted downturn in business, you reverse the process. You look at your organization and figure out where you have too much capacity; you eliminate that capacity from your futurized organization chart. I work with my clients to make certain that they always have a three- to five-year futurized organization chart that right-sizes their capacity to match with their goals. I also view a downturn in business as an opportunity to make capacity reductions that eliminate functional role individuals who are not meeting the rating level of 9. Many times, organizations are forced to retain a lower performing individual because the candidate market is so low that they cannot replace people with stronger new hires. Futurizing your organization for a downturn will provide you with an opportunity to keep the best performers through the downturn so that you will enter the upturn with a more highly rated organization.

The next step is to test whether or not the organization can afford these additional full-time employees and if they are financial smart decisions. Our example company currently generates fifty million in revenue with a net margin (sales less cost of goods sold less overhead) of 8 percent. They expect to hold that net margin as they grow the business. In order to grow the business, they need to add the people they identified in Figure 5.8 with the associated cost from Figure 5.2. Here's a quick and sure way to test the financial viability of adding capacity to the organization in order to achieve its growth goals:

Figure 5.9 Testing Financial Feasibility of Futurized Organization Chart

Description	Current Year	1st year	2nd year	3rd year
Revenue	$50,000,000	$60,000,000	$72,000,000	$82,800,000
Profit %	8 %	8 %	8 %	8 %
Profit	$4,000,000	$4,800,000	$5,800,000	$6,600,000
Number of Employees	72	88	101.5	116
Revenue per Employee	$694,444	$681,818	$709,360	$713,793
Profit per Employee	$55,555	$54,545	$57,142	$56,896*

By adding extra capacity in the first year, the organization has the capacity and capability to increase its revenues per employee and net margin per employee during the second year and third year. With this quick calculation, your group can validate that the added capacity and capability is a financially sound decision and plan. This calculation does not include the potential 32 percent gain in productivity that can be achieved by improving the organization's functional role delivery to a rating of 9.

*In year three, the profit per employee decreases. That is an indication that you might have added too much capacity, and it means that you and your executive team must reevaluate the added capacity in your futurized organization chart for year three. If the dollars per employee for revenue or profit decreases, you may have added too many employees or you may have underproductive employees who are not fulfilling their functional role requirements.

Once the futurized organization chart has been validated as financially feasible, the next step is to create job descriptions for each position, set the hiring requirements for each position, establish a budget for the salary and benefits for each position, and create a timetable for recruiting, hiring, and training the right people.

One of the other advantages of having a futurized organization chart is that it will identify whether or not you have enough space for everyone. Office space will be impacted by growth and knowing one to three years in advance of when you will need more space to house all of your employees will allow you ample time to complete an office space review. With that you can decide on either redesigning your current space or locating adequate space in a new location. This may also impact other areas of your business, such as your warehouse space for shipping, receiving, and inventory, as well as your production space for production lines and production equipment. Utilizing a space designer can help you get your future square footage calculated so that you can have the physical office, warehouse, and production capacity to achieve your growth goals.

Succession planning

Growth also puts a stress on leadership. Many times, organizations will grow and just add more people who report directly to the executive leadership team. This stretches the capability and capacity of any leader to a point where they will not be as effective as the organization needs them to be. As an organization grows, it also needs to develop its future leaders. The leader of each functional role needs to identify someone within their section of the organization chart who will be their successor. During growth phases, one of the major breakdowns in planning is making certain that there are enough leaders in the organization to take on the new responsibilities that are created by growth. The leaders of an organization need a succession plan. A common and accepted rule of leadership is that you should have no more than five direct reports. That allows you enough time to spend at least eight hours per week with each of your direct reports. In addition, the top leadership of an organization needs to spend time working on the immediate future. I define immediate future in a growing organization as being six to twelve months ahead. When the key leadership in an organization spends 100 percent of their time working on the day-to-day (tactical) activities of their functional role, they sacrifice the future of the entire organization. The key leadership, CEO, and the executive team need to have enough time to spend on planning for the immediate and longer-term future. If they are bogged down, spending 100 percent of their time in day-to-day activities, they will have no vision for the future

Each member of the executive team needs to identify a successor and adopt a plan that will provide the mentoring and skill development of the successor so that, at any time in the future, the executive can delegate some of their leadership responsibilities to their successor. The identification of a successor is necessary to sustain the strength of an organization. Without a strong successor plan in place, the organization will at some point exceed its capability and capacity to grow, resulting in chaos and the inability of the organization to achieve its strategic plan goals.

Chapter Six

Conclusion

Success Story: A Washington-based company developed a set of strategic plan goals during their planning session three years ago. They identified areas of weakness within their organization chart that would stifle their growth potential. They mapped out a plan for adding capability and capacity over a two-year period that would allow them to not only meet their goals but to exceed them. During the third year, they dominated their marketplace with growth that exceeded 25 percent per year in revenues and an equal 25 percent growth in profits. They saw an opportunity to expand their geographic areas as well as adding new product lines through two key acquisitions. Prior to the completion of the acquisitions, they futurized their organization chart to reflect the addition of two new acquisitions. They identified where they would need additional capabilities and capacity. They also added to their succession planning so that they could have the talent and skills required to absorb the two new companies and regions. The two acquisitions were completed in less than nine months. The chaos and confusion that could have resulted were eliminated because the acquired companies saw the futurized org chart and on how the acquisitions would be completed. No chaos, no confusion, just a well thought-out plan that was clearly communicated and successfully executed. In three years, this company grew from twenty-seven million to over one hundred million in revenues.

This is just one example of how my client companies have utilized the organizational alignment process in this book to power them forward in their marketplace with increased growth and profits from having an organizationally aligned company.

Growth and the changes it brings will stress your organization. Recognizing the current state of your organization and then mapping its future in an organized process mitigates the impact of that stress on your organization. No matter if the economy is in a growth cycle or in a downturn. Achieving organizational alignment is a process that identifies where your organization can improve. Achieving organizational alignment creates a plan for improving individuals, teams, and the overall organization. Futurizing your organization chart helps you identify where additional capability and capacity are required. By providing your organization with a visible path into the future, you eliminate the stress and chaos that are caused by growth. Having the capability and capacity within your organization will allow you to meet and exceed your strategic plan goals and sustain your organization's success well into the future.

The future is yours. Create your plan. Organize your team. Improve your performance by improving your teams and individuals. Then, write your own success story about how you and your team achieved organizational alignment and exceeded your strategic plan goals.

Appendix A:

Key Performance Indicators

Before you start working on your plans to achieve organizational alignment you need to examine measurements that you will use for checking the progress you are making toward achieving your strategic plan goals.

During your strategic planning session, you established realistic and achievable goals for your organization for the next five years. In my experience with over five hundred companies the most common strategic plan goals are:

- Revenues
- Gross margin
- Overhead expenses
- Profit

These financial goals are commonly referred to as Key Performance Indicators (KPIs) and should be used as benchmarks for evaluating your organization's performance. In addition to being benchmarks for your whole organization, KPIs should also be used as benchmarks for departments/teams/divisions and individuals.

As the CEO, along with your executive team, you need to identify what your key performance indicators are for your organization. You should be able to limit this to no more than five major key performance indicators. They should, in fact, be the same goals you set during your strategic planning retreat. Each of those major KPIs will have many subset data points. The subsets are important because they are used for evaluating team and individual performance. As in our example, the functional role description for sales was as follows:

> **Sales:** Responsible for achieving all sales goals including current client sales levels, increasing current client sales volumes, customer relationships, customer retention and adding new customers in order to reach the sales growth and gross margin goals of the company. Manages sales related overhead expenses.

The organization's KPIs that sales influences are: revenues and overhead expenses.

Let's say that the organization sells its products in several regions. A subset for the organization's revenue KPI for the sales functional role would be sales per region. A subset of regional sales would be sales by a sales representative. A subset of the sales per sales representative would be sales to existing customers and also sales to new customers. In this example, we have parsed out the revenue KPI for the company into regions, then sales representatives, existing customers, and finally into new customers. Here's how that looks from KPI through subsets:

KPI: Revenues

      Subset KPI: Regional sales

            Subset KPI: Sales by sales representative

                  Subset KPI: Sales to existing customers

                  Subset KPI: Sales to new customers

Using subsets, we have delegated the achievement of the KPI Revenue all the way down to an individual sales representative role. Using the KPIs and their subsets, we can now track individual performance, regional performance, and, ultimately, the organization's performance.

Figure 1 appendix is an example of the KPIs for an organization and some identified subsets of those KPIs.

Figure 1 Appendix: Key Performance Indicators and Subsets

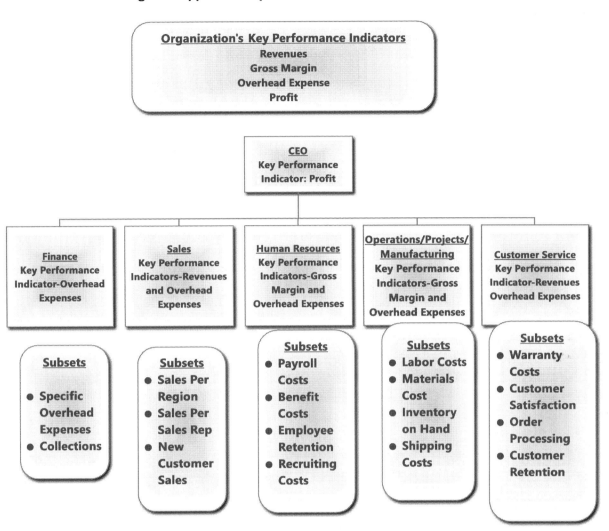

Take your organization's key performance indicators and convert them into functional role key performance indicators; this provides you with a management tool and a performance assessment tool to evaluate how a functional role is being performed all the way down to an individual employee.

Create your own hierarchy of key performance indicators and their subsets by starting with your five goals. Have your functional role managers (Figure 2.1 is an example of your functional role managers) create the subsets of the key performance indicators for their functional role group and for the individuals in their group. The important thing to remember is that each key performance indicator subset must have a relationship with the organization's three to five key performance indicators. If someone creates an unusual key performance indicator subset they must identify how it relates back to the organization's key performance indicators.

With your key performance indicators in place your organization can easily evaluate the progress it is making on improving the delivery of its functional roles. It is also easier to work with individuals and teams by having them measure their own progress on their achievement using the subsets of the key performance indicators. It is critical that you create your own KPIs and subsets so that you can work with individuals and teams to improve your organization's functional role delivery to a 9 rating.

Made in the USA
San Bernardino, CA
01 September 2016